KITE FLYING

KITE FLYING

by Dorothy Childers Schmitz

Library of Congress Catalog Card Number: 78-6876

International Standard Book Numbers:
0-913940-92-5 Library Bound
0-89686-013-2

Edited by - Dr. Howard Schroeder
Prof. in Reading and Language Arts
Dept. of Elementary Education
Mankato State University

Library of Congress
Cataloging in Publication Data

Schmitz, Dorothy Childers.
  Kite Flying

  (Funseekers)
  SUMMARY: A brief illustrated history of kites with a
description of various models, their construction, and their
uses.
  1. Kites--Juvenile literature.   (1. Kites)
I. Title.
TL759.5.S3   796.1'5   78-6876
ISBN 0-913940-92-5

PHOTO CREDITS

Photo Researchers Inc.: Cover, 3, 5, 7, 8, 10, 17, 18A, 18B, 19, 23, 25, 26, 27,
     28, 31, 32
Catherine Buckley, The Alberta Hang Gliding Assoc.: 14-15
Randal M. Heise: 22

KITE FLYING

KITE FLYING

It comes in many shapes and sizes. It can be any color you can imagine. It has been used for predicting the weather, spying on an enemy, lifting men and cargo, taking pictures, building bridges, advertising, sending signals, measuring distances, catching fish, lifesaving, celebrating, and for just having fun. What is it? A kite!

Most people know that the Chinese built and flew the first kites. But did you know that they probably did this as long ago as 1000 B.C.? There are many legends in Chinese folklore that tell about a great bird or a wooden bird that stayed in the air for many days. These tales are found in Japanese folklore as well. Knowledge of the kite probably spread from China to Japan, through the Buddhist missionaries.

Among these tales from the Orient are stories about man-carrying kites. If a man or woman was thought to have committed a crime, that person was strapped onto a kite and thrown out of a tower. If the kite landed safely, the person was allowed to go back home as if nothing had ever happened. A safe landing was proof of innocence. Most of the time, the landing ended in death for the passenger. This was thought to be proof of the person's guilt. So the punishment was "just."

A beautiful Chinese bird kite.

Another story tells of a father and his son who were exiled on an island. Their punishment was not to be able to set foot on the mainland again. The father wanted to get his son back to the mainland. So they built a kite of bamboo and pieces of their clothing. The legend says the kite carried the boy safely back to the mainland. There he was able to seek help for his father.

Many of the kites today are named after people in such legends. Others are painted and decorated as symbols during festivals and celebrations. During the Boys' Festival held every year in Japan, every family with a boy baby born that year flies a kite shaped like a carp. This fish symbol means that the son, like the carp, will progress through the river of his life.

Japanese carp kites flown during the Boys' Festival.

Scientists began using kites even before Benjamin Franklin did his famous experiment. In Scotland, two men fastened thermometers to kites and sent them up to record the temperature of the clouds. A few years later, Ben Franklin made a common kite from two crossed sticks covered with silk. He tied on some ordinary string, tied the key to the string, and waited for a thundercloud. He wanted to prove that lightning and electricity are the same thing. This experiment was done in June, 1752. His son was helping him with the experiment. They knew that if they were right, it could be a dangerous experiment. So they were careful to take cover inside the door. They also took care not to let the string touch the frame of the door. When the rain wet the kite and string, the key did conduct the electricity, and they knew that they were right.

Many other scientists have used kites in their experiments since that day. But none have become so famous as Ben Franklin and his kite.

Ben Franklin flying his famous kite.

Kites helped to build many bridges.

After the first experiments, scientists began to measure all kinds of things about weather. By 1900, they were able to measure temperature, moisture, wind speed, and barometric pressure. Later, these experiments were done from balloons and airplanes. Ben Franklin really started something! These early scientists set up an organization and called it the Franklin Kite Club. Today there are many such organizations for kite flyers.

Kites were also used in building bridges. Engineers used a kite to carry the cable across a river. A heavy cord was fastened to the kite string. The kite pulled the cord across the stream and settled in a tree. The process was repeated until a bridge was formed across the stream. Since then, many suspension bridges have been built using this method.

One of the most exciting missions for any kite is the spy mission. Douglas Archibald took the first known photographs from a kite. Since that time, cameras have been used to photograph enemy positions. The same methods are used in peace time to photograph cities, vacation spots, and cloud formations.

During World War II, a kite was part of the required equipment in life rafts. It was a signal to search parties. There are men alive today who owe their lives to a kite.

Did you ever want to fish off shore, but didn't have a boat? The fishing kite was invented by someone with the same problem. After the kite is launched, hook the fish line to the kite line. The fish line will travel out over the water and the bait will drop. When the fish strikes, the loop will break.

It was the kite and man's interest in finding new things to do with it that led to hang gliding and even to modern aviation. Even the Wright brothers did their first experiments with kites. They learned much of what they used in flight from their kite experiments.

There have been many people through the years who just wanted to have fun with a kite. There are so many ways to do just that. The sky is the limit!

Part of the fun of flying a kite is building it yourself. There are many different types. However, they all fall into either the basic flat type, or bowed type. The flat ones must have a tail. The bowed or angled ones do not. There are many combinations of the two.

The easiest ones to make are the flat kites. In making a flat kite, cross two sticks, make a string outline, cover with paper or cloth, add a tail, and you're ready to go.

The bowed kite is often called an Eddy, named after its inventor, William A. Eddy. Its two sticks are placed in a T-shape with a cross stick bowed toward the back. It does not need a tail. It's easy to make, is a good flier, and more steady than a flat kite.

The tetrahedral is called by that name because of its four sides. This makes it an angled kite. It is also a strong kite, and needs a strong wind to fly well.

The box kite is another of the angled kites. The box is formed by the oblong frame of four sticks with two cross braces at each end.

There are many kinds of novel shapes of kites that you can buy or build. The basic construction must be done with flying in mind. As long as the decoration does not hinder the flying of the kite, there is no end to what you can do to make your kite look like the best in the sky!

The finishing touches.

A winged box kite.

This one is called a tetrahedral kite.

The Chinese people have always wanted their kites to be the most beautiful, the most frightening, or the most durable, depending on the occasion. They are known for their beautiful designs which look so fragile but fly so well. The kites are shaped like snakes, dragons, butterflies, birds, and faces of gods and goddesses. Yet they fly like the sturdiest of kites. Many kite experts go to study their designs and learn their secrets of kite flying.

The Chinese people have designed many fantastic kites.

After you have built your kite, you will want to have some fun with it. You will discover that there is much more to kite flying than just getting it into the air and then watching it fly. What fun can be had by flying your kite with a little imagination! Add a windmill to your kite and watch it go. Or try to whistle, and listen to the sound effects as you launch your kite. There are some rules to remember when adding things to your kite. Never drive nails or tacks through the sticks. They may split under pressure. Tying with string many times over gives more strength than by using heavier twine.

There are some safety rules to remember, too. The following is a code for flying a kite:

- Never use wire, nails, tack staples or anything metal in your kite.
- Never fly your kite near utility wires, high-voltage wires, or transmission towers.
- Never try to remove a kite from an electric wire or high pole.
- Never fly a kite on or over a public street or road.
- Never fly your kite in a thunderstorm.
- Never use wet string or a wire for a line.

Flying a kite is one of the safest things you can do for fun. Observing these simple rules will make it even more safe.

BUILD YOUR OWN KITE
(Follow these easy directions)

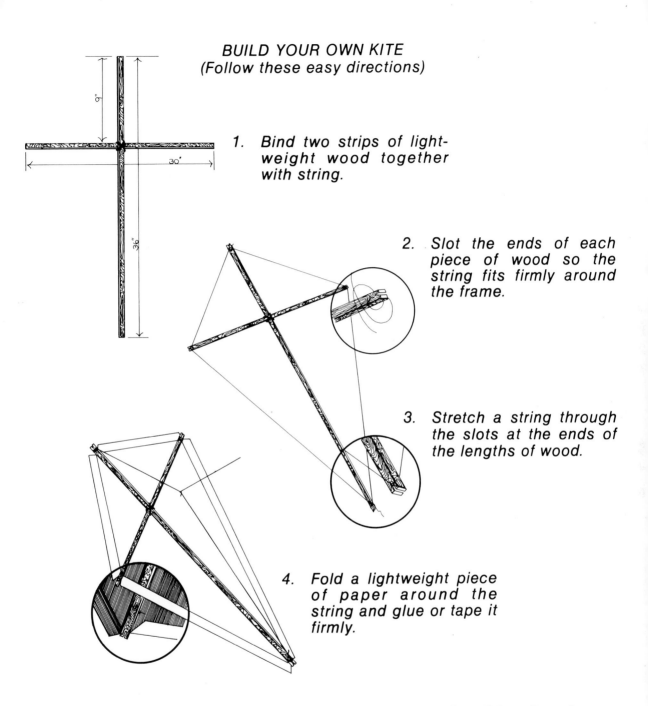

1. Bind two strips of light-weight wood together with string.

2. Slot the ends of each piece of wood so the string fits firmly around the frame.

3. Stretch a string through the slots at the ends of the lengths of wood.

4. Fold a lightweight piece of paper around the string and glue or tape it firmly.

5. Attach bridle string to ends of longest part of frame. Attach flying string to bridle at point where frame sticks cross.

6. Now add a 3 to 5 ft. tail made of lightweight material. This will make the kite fly much better.

Ready? Let's get that kite into the air! The ideal place to fly your kite is a big, open field with no wires, houses, or trees. If you have such a place, all you need is a little wind. You will need at least a four-mile-an-hour wind. There is a simple way to measure the speed of the wind:

- 4 to 7 miles per hour - leaves rustle lightly on the trees
- 8 to 12 miles per hour - tree leaves will stay in motion
- 13 to 18 miles per hour - tops of trees bend
- 19 to 24 miles per hour - small trees sway

In a four-mile-an-hour wind, the very lightest kite will fly. However, eight to fifteen miles per hour is best. Most kites are strong enough to stand winds up to twenty miles per hour. If winds are greater than twenty-four miles per hour, special kite construction and experience in flying in strong wind are both needed. It isn't much fun to build a kite and then lose it to a too strong wind. Wait until conditions are right for your kite.

"Go fly a kite."

Let's say that the wind is right and you are ready to fly. If you have a friend to help, the launching will be much easier. Send your friend downwind. A small kite will need between fifty to one hundred feet of slack in the string. A larger kite may need up to one hundred yards. Have your friend hold the kite off the ground. The tail of the kite is for balance. Be sure that it serves its purpose. To do so, it must be spread out on the ground behind the kite. If the tail is laid out downwind, the kite gets the balance it needs in the first few feet of rise. If you have enough breeze, you will not need to run after it reaches a certain height. It is possible to launch a kite without a helper, but much easier and more fun, too, to share your fun with a friend.

Now your kite is off the ground. You can feel the pull and tug of the wind as it reaches a level of stronger wind. If your kite has reached the proper angle to the wind, it will probably stay there until you decide to pull it in. Without that angle, it may wobble, spin, or even dive suddenly to the ground. A good stiff breeze may show you what is wrong with your kite. If it suddenly jerks, wobbles, spins, or dives, bring it in and look it over. It's better to have a chance to make little repairs than to rebuild.

Al Hartig, famous kite designer, flys one of his masterpieces on the beach of Nantucket, Maine.

24

Trees and kites don't mix.

A hole torn in the cover will make the kite fly lop-sided. A stick moved out of position will throw the kite out of balance. If you have the things you need to fix your kite close at hand, you will be back in the air in no time. A first aid kite kit should contain a knife or scissors, some tape, glue, and string.

What if that friend, who was helping you, launches his own kite? Challenge him to a friendly bat-tle. Kite fighting is probably as old as kite flying. You and your opponent will have to agree to do battle and set up the ground rules in advance. Some of the Chinese kites go into battle with ground glass glued onto the cord. The attack kite then tries to saw through the cord of the other kite. The one who is able to saw through first is the winner. The loser's kite then belongs to the winner. This has to be agreed upon before the battle, of course.

Fly a message over the territory of a friend. This is done the same way the advertisers do it. Just attach your streamer to each side of the kite so as not to upset the balance. Write the message across the streamers in large, clear letters, launch your kite and deliver your message!

If you want to have some real fun on the ice some winter afternoon, attach a small sled to your largest kite. If the ice is smooth, you may be amazed at the ease with which your kite will pull the sled. Of course, you will have checked out the usual dangers of kite flying as well as those for ice skating. Don't be on the ice if it isn't completely safe. If all conditions are right for ice sledding and for kite flying, it can be an afternoon of great fun for the kite-flying sled passenger!

After you get into building and flying your own kites, you will think of many things to do with them. You and your friends may find kite flying to be a favorite way to spend an afternoon.

All over the country, there are people, young and old, who share your fun. The American Kiteflyers Association now has members in local chapters in every state and twenty-six countries. They publish a newsletter called *KITE TALES*. If you would like more information, write to the association at this address:

American Kiteflyers Association
P.O. Box 1511
Silver City, New Mexico 88061

The next time anyone says to you, "Go fly a kite!", you may have a different answer. Maybe you'll say, "Yes, I believe I will! It's a lot of fun! Do you want to come along?"